Nashua Public Library

Enjoy this book!

Please remember to return it on time
so that others may enjoy it too.

Manage your library account and
discover all we offer by visiting us
online at www.nashualibrary.org

Love your library? Tell a friend!

J

FREAKY PHENOMENA

FAITH

FREAKY PHENOMENA

The Series

CONSCIOUSNESS
FAITH
HEALING
LIFE AFTER DEATH
MYSTERIOUS PLACES
PERSONALITY
PSYCHIC ABILITIES
THE SENSES

FREAKY PHENOMENA

FAITH

Don Rauf

Foreword by Joe Nickell, Senior Research Fellow, Committee for Skeptical Inquiry

MASON CREST

Mason Crest
450 Parkway Drive, Suite D Broomall, PA 19008
www.masoncrest.com

Copyright © 2018 by Mason Crest, an imprint of National Highlights, Inc. All rights reserved. No part of this publication may be reproduced or transmitted in any form or by any means, electronic or mechanical, including photocopying, recording, taping, or any information storage and retrieval system, without permission in writing from the publisher.

Printed in the United States of America

First printing
9 8 7 6 5 4 3 2 1

Series ISBN: 978-1-4222-3772-4
Hardcover ISBN: 978-1-4222-3774-8
ebook ISBN: 978-1-4222-8008-9

Cataloging-in-Publication Data is available on file at the Library of Congress.

Developed and Produced by Print Matters Productions, Inc. (www.printmattersinc.com)
Cover and Interior Design by: Bill Madrid, Madrid Design
Composition by Carling Design

Picture credits: 9, Matt_Gibson/iStock; 10, Tatiana Ganapolsskaya/Shutterstock; 12, jasminam/iStock; 13, lowellgordon/iStock; 16, Roman Sigaev/Shutterstock; 19, ZU_09/iStock; 20, Renata Sedmakova/Shutterstock; 21, By Philippe Plet.via Wikimedia Commons; 22, sedmak/iStock; 24, udra11/Shutterstock; 25, National Institute of Mental Health; 26, nutech21/Shutterstock; 29, ljubaphoto/iStock; 30, iStock; 32, THEPALMER/iStock; 35, watcharakun/Shutterstock; 36, Dudarev Mikhail/Shutterstock, John Faed via Wikimedia Commons; 38, Freedom Studio/Shutterstock; 41, annegeorg/iStock; 42, gemphoto/Shutterstock

Cover: umbertoleporini/iStock

CONTENTS

KEY ICONS TO LOOK FOR:

Words to Understand: These words with their easy-to-understand definitions will increase the reader's understanding of the text, while building vocabulary skills.

Sidebars: This boxed material within the main text allows readers to build knowledge, gain insights, explore possibilities, and broaden their perspectives by weaving together additional information to provide realistic and holistic perspectives.

Research Projects: Readers are pointed toward areas of further inquiry connected to each chapter. Suggestions are provided for projects that encourage deeper research and analysis.

Series glossary of key terms: This back-of-the book glossary contains terminology used throughout this series. Words found here increase the reader's ability to read and comprehend higher-level books and articles in this field.

Advice From a Full-Time Professional Investigator of Strange Mysteries

I wish I'd had books like this when I was young. Like other boys and girls, I was intrigued by ghosts, monsters, and other freaky things. I grew up to become a stage magician and private detective, as well as (among other things) a literary and folklore scholar and a forensic-science writer. By 1995, I was using my varied background as the world's only full-time professional investigator of strange mysteries.

As I travel around the world, lured by its enigmas, I avoid both uncritical belief and outright dismissal. I insist mysteries should be *investigated* with the intent of solving them. That requires *critical thinking*, which begins by asking useful questions. I share three such questions here, applied to brief cases from my own files:

Is a particular story really true?

Consider Louisiana's Myrtles Plantation, supposedly haunted by the ghost of a murderous slave, Chloe. We are told that, as revenge against a cruel master, she poisoned three members of his family. Phenomena that ghost hunters attributed to her spirit included a mysteriously swinging door and unexplained banging noises.

The Discovery TV Channel arranged for me to spend a night there alone. I learned from the local historical society that Chloe never existed and her three alleged victims actually died in a yellow fever epidemic. I prowled the house, discovering that the spooky door was simply hung off center, and that banging noises were easily explained by a loose shutter.

Does a claim involve unnecessary assumptions?

In Flatwoods, WV, in 1952, some boys saw a fiery UFO streak across the evening sky and apparently land on a hill. They went looking for it, joined by others. A flashlight soon revealed a tall creature with shining eyes and a face shaped like the ace of spades. Suddenly, it swooped at them with "terrible claws," making a high-pitched hissing sound. The witnesses fled for their lives.

Half a century later, I talked with elderly residents, examined old newspaper accounts, and did other research. I learned the UFO had been a meteor. Descriptions of the creature almost perfectly matched a barn owl—seemingly tall because it had perched on a tree limb. In contrast, numerous incredible assumptions would be required to argue for a flying saucer and an alien being.

Is the proof as great as the claim?

A Canadian woman sometimes exhibited the crucifixion wounds of Jesus—allegedly produced supernaturally. In 2002, I watched blood stream from her hands and feet and from tiny scalp wounds like those from a crown of thorns.

However, because her wounds were already bleeding, they could have been self-inflicted. The lance wound that pierced Jesus' side was absent, and the supposed nail wounds did not pass through the hands and feet, being only on one side of each. Getting a closer look, I saw that one hand wound was only a small slit, not a large puncture wound. Therefore, this extraordinary claim lacked the extraordinary proof required.

These three questions should prove helpful in approaching claims and tales in Freaky Phenomena. I view the progress of science as a continuing series of solved mysteries. Perhaps you too might consider a career as a science detective. You can get started right here.

Joe Nickell
Senior Research Fellow, Committee for Skeptical Inquiry
Amherst, NY

Believing In A Higher Power

People with a strong belief in God often believe that their faith and devotion to a higher power can provide them with answers, help, and even miracles. The early Christian philosopher St. Augustine said, "Faith is to believe what you do not see; the reward of this faith is to see what you believe."

For some, faith and positive thinking are closely related although not the same. The minster Norman Vincent Peale made a career promoting both. With psychoanalyst Smiley Blanton, Peale cowrote *Faith Is the Answer: A Psychiatrist and Pastor Discuss Your Problems* (1940). Peale's most popular book is *The Power of Positive Thinking*. Some distinguish between the two ideas saying that faith is submitting to God's will, whereas positive thinking is a "self-willing" and wishing for a desire to come true. For many, a strong belief in God can lead to miracles and supernatural occurrences.

In 2013, 22-year-old Morgan Lake was driving along the Chesapeake Bay Bridge in Virginia on a beautiful summer night. Moments after she came to a stop for a toll, a large truck slammed into her from behind, sending Morgan and her vehicle off the bridge and plummeting into the water below. Water rushed into her car. Morgan struggled with the seatbelt but could not get it to open. In her mind, she reached out to God. She felt that God touched her; told her to relax. She could then release the safety belt. She rose up out of the driver's side window and swam to the surface. For Morgan, her faith saved her.

Some who have a deep belief in the spiritual world have had visitations or visions of angels. Others believe in the power of faith to heal, or that God can give revelations about the future (prophecies). On a darker side, could the Devil cause inexplicable and sinister occurrences on Earth? Many tales have been told of souls who have been possessed by the Devil—speaking gibberish, writhing in bed, or exhibiting other strange or violent behavior. This volume of *Freaky Phenomena* takes a look at some of the mysteries humans have experienced related to faith.

CHAPTER 1

ANGELS

The belief in guardian angels can be traced back for centuries. Some have described a mysterious person, or a great light, whereas others have described a distinct presence. No matter the form, thousands of people swear that these entities are real.

March 2015, an 18-month-old girl, Lily Groesbeck, was dramatically rescued from a car wreck. Her mother had lost control of the car and crashed into the icy Spanish Fork River in Salt Lake City, UT. Somehow, the toddler survived 14 hours in an overturned Dodge sedan that was partially submerged in the cold waters. When four police officers arrived at the scene, they heard an adult female voice calling, "Help me, help me." When they got into the car, they were surprised to find that the 25-year-old mother was long dead—yet they had all distinctly heard a voice crying for help. Although little Lily was unconscious and suffering from **hypothermia**, she was alive and made a full recovery in the hospital.

Who then called out? Video footage even captures a muffled voice. Was the voice her mother communicating after death? One officer said it had to be the voice of a heavenly **guardian**. Are such beings real or can they be explained as some mysterious side of our consciousness that helps us in times of need or crisis?

Angels are spiritual beings. The name angel comes from Greek for "messenger." Angels are often thought to be messengers or agents of God who may be sent to Earth to guide or comfort people during a troubling time. They are **paraphysical** entities—having some sort of physical presence but also having a nonphysical dimension. According to the Bible, angels are "ministering spirits" (Hebrews

Words to Understand

Celestial: Relating to the sky or heavens.

Divine: Relating to God or a god.

Guardian: A protector or defender.

Hypothermia: A condition of having a body temperature that is dangerously low.

Paraphysical: Not part of the physical word; often used in relation to supernatural occurrences.

Guardian Angels

St. Thomas Aquinas, the 13th-century Italian priest and philosopher, wrote that "from the very moment of his birth man has an angel guardian appointed to him." Almost all religions have a concept that each individual is assigned a type of spirit guide to help them through life. Ancient Sanskrit writings refer to angels and angiras (Hindu supernatural beings). In early Mesopotamia (3200 BC–539 BC), a former region in the eastern Mediterranean, people believed in beings called the shedu and the lamassu who protected them. Ancient Egypt's hierarchy of neteru (gods/goddesses) has been compared to Christianity's angels. Islam states that every person is protected by two angels. In Hebrew, malakh is the word for angel and basically means "messenger." The Buddhist equivalent of angels is devas, or **celestial** beings.

In ancient Mesopotamia, the lamassu was depicted as having a human head, a body of an ox or a lion, and a bird's wings.

1:14). God sends the angels to help man bring about God's will. In the Bible, they deliver the news of the birth of Jesus. From early days of Christian history, angels have been depicted as having wings and halos. But in reports of contact with spiritual guardians, these entities are often a presence without a definite form.

The Scientific Take: The Third Man Factor

This sensing of an unexplained presence has been reported many times throughout history. Scientists call the phenomenon "The Third Man Factor." Often the sensation that a guardian or angel is present to a person occurs in extreme survival situations. One theory is that in moments of severe stress, trauma, or sleep deprivation, the brain may have a coping mechanism that produces an inner, imagined character who provides comfort. Studies performed on people with brain injuries have found that when an area of the brain called the temporoparietal junction is stimulated with an electrical current, the patient may sense "a presence" that is not there. When the brain is affected in a traumatic manner, it may create an autoscopic experience, which means one feels that a representation of one's own body has been projected outside the self.

After Ernest Shackleton and his men got stuck in the ice during their 1916 Antarctic expedition, three of them trekked across glaciers and mountain ranges to get help. All of the men reported feeling a "**divine**" presence with them—a spirit assuring their safe passage.

Find out more about the Third Man Factor.

The remains of Sir Ernest Shackleton's ship. Just six years after his experience with the divine, Shackleton passed away while on his final expedition.

Two days after the horrific terrorist attacks in New York City, an excavator spotted a sign of hope amid chaos. A cross, formed from the towers' fallen steel beams, stood strong on Ground Zero. It remains intact, a part of the National September 11 Memorial & Museum.

In World War I, British Royal Navy commander Harry Stoker and two other comrades made a daring escape from a Turkish prison. They traveled hundreds of miles across the rugged Taurus Mountains through intense cold. Stoker later wrote that he always felt four people were struggling along rather than three. He saw the invisible fourth presence as a loyal friend who was saying, "I cannot help, but when danger is at hand remember always that I am here, to stand—or fall—with you."

When a jet hijacked by terrorists struck the second tower at the World Trade Center in 2001, Ron DiFrancesco felt trapped above floors that were consumed with smoke and flames. But at one desperate point, he says he sensed an angel who urged him on. He felt a presence that "led me to the stairwell, led me to break through, led me to run through the fire." He felt that someone had guided him, that "somebody lifted me up." He was able to make it past the flames and eventually out to safety before the tower collapsed.

Angels Save a Classroom

On May 16, 1986, an unhinged man and his wife took 136 children and 4 adults hostage at an elementary school in Cokeville, WY. The man demanded a ransom of $2 million per hostage. If they did not get it, they would set off a bomb. When the homemade bomb accidentally went off, none of the children were hurt. Moments before it exploded, they moved toward the windows. After the episode, a few of the children said that angels appeared to them. Here is how one child described it:

> I was sitting in the classroom playing with a toy when something made me look up. That's when I saw the angels. They were shiny, with flowing white robes. Some were holding hands. They glided down through the ceiling, then hung in the air for a second. I felt totally safe. Everyone seemed to have an angel. They came down next to us. My angel was a beautiful shining woman. It was almost as if she landed on my shoulder. She said, 'Don't be scared, Nathan. Get up and go to the window. The bomb is about to go off.' I did just what she said. Other children started doing the same thing.

CHAPTER 2

STIGMATA

"So the soldiers took charge of Jesus. Carrying his own cross, he went out to the place of the Skull. There they crucified him, and with him two others—one on each side and Jesus in the middle."
—John 19:16-18

Throughout history, a large number of Christians (mostly Roman Catholics) have experienced an inexplicable physical phenomenon called the stigmata. The word stigma itself means "mark," and stigmata is a mystical experience whereby a believer in Christ mysteriously becomes physically imprinted with the wounds of Christ. Body marks, sores, or sensations of pain appear that correspond with the lacerations and other trauma endured during the crucifixion. These marks may resemble the Lord's spike wounds to his feet and hands, scratches to the head where He wore a crown of thorns, an injury to the side of the torso close to the heart matching the bodily damage from a Roman soldier's lance, and possibly whip marks on the back. The Catholic Education Resource Center says that a genuine stigmatic bleeds from the wounds, especially on the day when believers remember the Lord's sacrifice—Fridays and particularly Good Friday.

Many of those with stigmata are described as **ecstatics** who are overwhelmed with emotion. A few have claimed to have an invisible stigmata; they have only the pain where the wounds would be but no visible marks. A large number live on very little food.

Words to Understand

Ecstatic: A person subject to mystical experiences.

Elation: Great happiness.

Hysteric: Characterized by uncontrollable laughing.

Inflammation: A reaction that produces swelling, redness, and pain as a result of infection, irritation, or injury.

Malignant: Likely to grow and spread in a fast and uncontrolled way that can cause death.

Sanctity: A state or quality of holiness.

Hundreds of Cases
Ted Harrison, a former religious correspondent for the BBC, estimates that since the year 1224 there have been over 400 reported cases of stigmata.

The Scientific Take: A Physical Phenomenon

In the scientific realm, wounds labeled as stigmata do not just appear magically. There is some sort of physical cause at the root. Some researchers have attributed the marks to self-starvation or self-mutilation. Studies of prisoners of war and famine victims have shown that trauma may lead to an unconscious self-mutilation. Other cases of divine stigmata were proven to be hoaxes—wounds inflicted to gain attention. Some investigations of stigmatics have shown that their marks may have been caused by disease (as may have been the case of St. Francis—see next page). However, some scientists believe that a person who is distraught or hysterical may have a physical reaction caused by their mind. In the book *Psychic Oddities,* Hereward Carrington cites a case where a person is surprised by a burglar. The burglar does not touch the person, but he believes the burglar has grabbed his arm. Later, the person finds that his arm is mysteriously bruised. Action in the brain can possibly produce a reaction on the skin.

The First Stigmata

St. Francis of Assisi was the first recorded case of stigmata. In 1224, when a six-winged angel who was crucified allegedly appeared before him, St. Francis experienced feelings of **elation** combined with pain and suffering. When the vision vanished, he was left with wounds to his feet, hands, and side. Hundreds of years later, researchers studied St. Francis's health problems. In 1935, a Dr. Edward Frederick Hartung concluded that the holy man suffered from an eye infection contracted in Egypt and died at age 45 from **malignant** malaria. Based on this analysis, St. Francis's stigmata might have actually

Learn more about the history of stigmata.

St. Francis of Assisi, a core figure within Catholicism, was the first recorded case of stigmata.

been the result of this type of malaria, known to cause purpura, or a purple hemorrhage of blood in the skin.

Dramatic Cases

On September 20, 1918, Padre Pio of Pietrelcina in Italy received visible stigmata, which remained with him for the following 50 years of his life. He supposedly lost one cup of blood every day. Physicians examined his wounds but could make no diagnosis—they commented on the remarkable smooth edges of the marks and the lack of **inflammation**. The bloody openings also gave off a sweet smell called the "odor of **sanctity**" instead of the smell of blood. The wounds caused Padre Pio intense pain, which was greatly heightened when he was celebrating Mass. One physician explained that his wounds were self-inflicted, and the father was a

Although the subject of his stigmata was controversial, many looked to Padre Pio of Pietrelcina's wounds as evidence of holiness.

hysteric. Shortly after his death, his stigmata disappeared and reportedly his skin was unblemished.

Gemma Galgani (1878–1903), a Catholic saint from Italy, had stigmata that only appeared on a weekly basis. On Thursday nights, she would go into a state of ecstasy. Then marks as if from a crown of thorns would appear on her head. By noon on Friday, wounds would open on her feet and hands and she would be bleeding profusely. By Saturday, however, the wounds would be completely healed with just slight white scarring left behind.

The Italian Catholic mystic Natuzza Evolo (1924–2009) had a very strange form of stigmata. The blood that dripped from her stigmata miraculously formed Christian writing, images, or symbols on bandages and other types of cloth. Often the words were in Hebrew or the ancient language of Aramaic.

Miraculously cured of spinal meningitis, Gemma was passionate about spreading the word, and claimed to have seen guardian angels and Jesus, daily.

CHAPTER 3

POSSESSION AND EXORCISM

Early writings depict the symbolic battle of the soul with demons.

W hile those who maintain a firm belief in the spiritual world may believe in forces of good that are at work to guide us through life, many also believe in forces of evil. There are those who are certain that the Devil and demons are carrying on all sorts of mischief and **mayhem** on this earth.

The idea that evil spirits can possess people exists in many different faiths. It's a belief that goes back to ancient times and continues to this day. When someone is possessed, it is generally thought that a **malevolent** spirit has taken over that person's mind and body to one degree or another. In certain Native American cultures, however, it is believed that a shaman (healer) could be temporarily possessed by spirits with supernatural powers who can help heal people.

A belief in possession by evil forces can be found in Christianity, Judaism, Islam, Buddhism, Hinduism, and other religions. The ancient Sumerians thought that all diseases of the body and mind were caused by "sickness demons" called gidim or gid-dim. There are six times in the Bible when Jesus casts out demons. In today's Western culture, possession may be most closely tied to the Christian religion, because of its depiction in The Exorcist and other horror movies. The exorcism is the religious ceremony conducted to expel the evil spirit from a person's body. (Strangely enough, possession seems to affect teens more than other age groups, although many parents may think sinister teen behavior is to be expected.)

Words to Understand

Catatonic: To be in a daze or stupor.

Malevolent: Evil.

Mayhem: Chaos.

Tourette syndrome: a disorder of tics, involuntary repetitive movements, and vocalizations.

Those possessed by something wicked may appear to have animalistic or crude behaviors.

A person who is thought to be possessed may exhibit uncharacteristic aggressiveness, be more sexual, spit, curse, laugh hysterically, hear voices, vomit, or speak in gibberish. One might hear multiple voices coming out of the possessed person. On the other hand, one possessed can go into a **catatonic** state, stare straight ahead, and barely blink. An individual suspected of being possessed may avoid or be repelled by churches, holy water, and the cross. Believers in possession think the eyes might change (since they are thought to be the windows to the soul). In extreme cases, the body may twist into seemingly impossible positions. The afflicted may reportedly gain superhuman strength and even telepathic powers—an ability to read minds—or possibly the ability of precognition, a knowing of future events. There have been some accounts where the possessed individual levitated.

Explore the history of possessions and exorcisms.

The Scientific Take: Possession Is Not a Medical Condition

Doctors do not recognize demonic possession as an official medical or psychiatric condition. It is not listed in the American Psychiatric Association's Diagnostic and Statistical Manual of Mental Disorders. Most of the symptoms can be attributed to mental illness. The symptoms are linked to hysteria, mania, psychosis, schizophrenia, **Tourette syndrome**, and other mental disorders. A person with schizophrenia might believe that he or she is hearing the voice of Satan. Their feelings of possession may be delusions or hallucinations. Seizures of epilepsy and odd behaviors from drug abuse or brain injury may also be interpreted as possession.

This composite MRI (magnetic resonance imaging) scan of the brain was created by the National Institute of Mental Health. It shows areas of gray matter lost over five years, comparing normal teens (left) and teens with childhood onset schizophrenia (right). The red and yellow denote areas of greater loss. Schizophrenia symptoms are often mistaken for demonic possession.

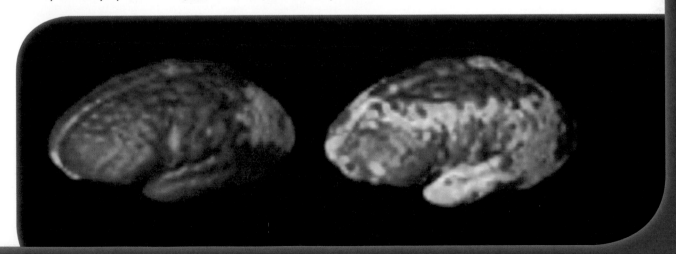

For an exorcism, priests invoke God's will and drive out the evil entity in the name of Jesus. One scientific theory is that a person undergoing an exorcism may enter a hypnotic state during which they are prone to the power of suggestion. Through this hypnosis, the possessed is able to change behaviors and believe that demons have left their body. (Dr. Peter R. Berwick of Arizona writes about this in *The American Journal of Clinical Hypnosis*.)

Call an Exorcist

The word exorcism actually comes from the Greek word for "oath." The process involves something similar to placing the invading demon under a type of "oath" that commands the evil spirit to leave the body. Once a demon is detected as possessing someone, the demon may be tricky and try to hide. When priests force a demon to reveal itself, it may talk through the possessed, and then the exorcist and the demon engage in a battle of good versus evil.

Although not every exorcism is successful, there have been victories. When many people think of exorcism, they think of the 1973 movie *The Exorcist*. The film was based on the story of a 13-year-old boy named Robbie Mannheim from Cottage City, MD. He was known to be a quiet and studious young man from a very ordinary family. Things changed in the summer of 1948

Although Ouija boards can be used for fun and games, they bring about a sense of fear in many who use them.

when his aunt showed him how to use a Ouija board, a popular novelty item through which some people believe they can communicate with the dead.

Not long after, the aunt died of natural causes, and strange things began to happen in the Mannheim home: The family heard unusual banging sounds in the basement and witnessed the chandelier swinging on its own accord. A portrait of Jesus moved without anyone touching it. Unexplained noises and movements continued in the house, and one day the mother walked into Robbie's bedroom and found the entire bed violently shaking with him in it. The mysterious occurrences escalated with night tables, dressers, and coffee tables suddenly moving. Meanwhile, Robbie began to get unexplained bruises, welts, and scratches on his body.

After the parents took the child to therapists who could find nothing wrong with the boy, they decided to consult a priest, Father Albert Hughes. In his first face-to-face meeting with the boy, Father Hughes said his chair suddenly levitated, and he was thrown against the wall. The father asked the boy in Latin: "What is your name?" He replied: "I am legions." Seeing the boy understand his question, the priest now thought he was talking directly to multiple diabolical entities within Robbie.

The boy's condition grew rapidly more erratic. He began rocking, spitting, and screaming. Because he had become increasingly more violent, Robbie was admitted to a hospital where nurses strapped him to a bed. The family agreed that an exorcism should be performed. Over the course of three days, Father Hughes recited exorcism prayers over the boy but they had no effect. He became increasingly agitated, and one night Robbie broke free of the constraints. He reached under the bed, ripped out a spring, and slashed the priest on the arm, creating a bloody gash that required 100 stitches. Father Hughes felt he was unable to help.

According to one account, the words "St. Louis" then appeared mysteriously on the boy's chest. The family took it as a sign, and they moved Robbie to that city where a Father William Bowdern performed a process of exorcism over a six-week period. The boy continued to be vulgar and violent, almost possessing superhuman strength. During one visit, he took a swing and broke Father Bowdern's nose.

The priest thought if the boy could be baptized and then receive Communion, that by eating the Communion wafer, he might be cured. Robbie's resistance escalated, but with the assistance of another priest, Father Bowdern was finally able to get him to take Communion. A few days later he spoke in a normal voice: "Satan! Satan! I am Saint Michael, and I command you, Satan and the other evil spirits, to leave the body now."

From that point on, Robbie steadily grew calmer. He attended Mass. He returned to his old self. The family and priests were convinced the exorcism had worked, and Robbie returned to a normal life in Maryland. He went on, without episode, to get married, and have children and grandchildren—the demons never returned.

More Tales of Possession and Cures

Anna Ecklund was another teen who was thought to be possessed by the Devil. Her story was made famous in the book *Begone Satan* by the German priest, the Reverend Father Carl Vogl. In 1896, the 14-year-old girl from Iowa spewed lewd language and demonstrated a repulsion to all religious items. She showed the signs of possession into early adulthood and it wasn't until she was 30 that she had her first exorcism. A monk in Wisconsin was said to successfully carry out the ritual, but when she was 46 her demons returned.

She was taken to a convent to again exorcise the evil spirits. Nuns tried to give her food that they blessed, but she would refuse it. She hissed like a wild cat and vomited foul substances. Some say she suddenly cursed in Latin, taunted the nuns, displayed abnormal strength, and even levitated. After 23 days of having rituals performed over her to rid her of these spirits, Ecklund awoke clear-minded and thanking Jesus. The entities had apparently been expelled from her body, never to return again.

In South Africa in 1906, Clara Germana Cele confessed to a priest that at age 16 she had made a pact with the devil. A nun wrote that Cele could speak several languages even though she had never learned them. She seemed to be able to read minds, she was repulsed by religious

The Bible and crucifixes are common objects used by priests during an exorcism.

objects, and she violently pushed nuns away from her. Cele even ripped off her clothes and growled. An attending nun wrote: "No animal had ever made such sounds. Neither the lions of East Africa nor the angry bulls. At times, it sounded like a veritable herd of wild beasts orchestrated by Satan had formed a hellish choir." When sprinkled with holy water, she occasionally levitated, according to some eyewitness accounts. A bite she gave to one nun was said to look like a serpent. For two days, two Roman Catholic priests performed an exorcism and drove the demons from her body.

Exorcism as Abuse

Some who have performed exorcisms have been accused of abuse. Some of the procedures can be violent and harmful. In 2011, an Indiana woman was convicted of killing her two-year-old son after forcing him to drink a concoction of olive oil and vinegar that she thought would rid him of a demon.

Pope Francis—the current pope of the Catholic Church.

In Milwaukee in 2003, an autistic eight-year-old boy died while wrapped in sheets during a prayer service held to exorcise the evil spirits that church members blamed for his condition. On Christmas Day 2010 in an East London high rise, a 15-year-old boy named Kristy Bamu was beaten and drowned by relatives trying to exorcise an evil spirit from the boy.

The granddaughter of acclaimed actor Morgan Freeman was stabbed to death on a Manhattan sidewalk in what witnesses described as an "exorcism" at the hands of her ranting boyfriend. Attempts at personal exorcism cannot replace the proven methods of psychiatric therapy.

The Catholic Church's Position

Today's Catholic Church still believes in the possibility of exorcism and possession. Pope Francis upholds that the Devil is active in this world and tempts people to stray from their faith. Some Catholics have said that Pope Francis has raised awareness of Satan and the dark arts, and this in turn has led to increasing reports of possession.

In spring of 2015, 160 Catholic priests from around the world gathered in Rome for a week-long exorcism conference endorsed by the Vatican. A British exorcist priest who attended but wished to remain aonymous said on Catholic Online:

> Some people are mentally ill and do not need exorcism. However, others do and there are some classic signs—people who speak in ancient tongues, for instance. Other people have supernatural strength when they are in a state of possession—it might take four men to hold down a slightly built woman. In some cases, people are able to levitate.

The late Father Gabriele Amorth, who styled himself as a "Satan buster," served as the official exorcist of Rome and claimed to have performed 160,000 exorcisms. One of his most dramatic occurred within the walls of the Vatican. In 2000, a 19-year-old girl appeared before Pope John Paul II and began to spew obscenities. They tried to rid the girl of her evil, but she fled the Vatican still controlled by a demon.

Channeling

Channeling is a form of possession in which the dead or spirits are thought to be able to be summoned and enter a person's body. Someone with the ability to call a spirit into his or her body is called a medium. Through the medium, the spirit may speak. Some mediums are said to use "spirit guides" who can help them communicate with the dead. The guide helps find a dead person's energy field and then delivers a message to the living through the medium, who may go into a trance to reach the spirit. The difference between possession and channeling: possession is an unwelcome invasion, while channeling is an invitation. Possession is also harmful, whereas channeling is generally used to find wisdom and peace.

CHAPTER 4

PROPHECY

During the 40-year journey to the Promised Land, Moses led the Israelites to Mount Sinai, where he was given the Ten Commandments from God. These now play a fundamental role in Christianity and Judaism.

Many people of different faiths who believe in God believe there are prophets on Earth. A prophet communicates with God and tells others what God said. Prophecy is sometimes called "divine inspiration." Many Christians say that Jesus was not only the son of God but also a prophet. Muhammad was the prophet who founded Islam.

Prophecies are messages from God that **predict** the future. In the Bible, God commanded Moses to free the Jews from slavery in Egypt. He fulfilled God's wishes, leading the people through 40 years of wandering in the desert to finally arrive at the edge of the Promised Land. Christians believe he foretold the coming of Jesus saying, "The Lord your God will raise up for you a prophet like me from among you, from your countrymen, you shall listen to him."

Many Mormons contend that the religion's founder and first prophet, Joseph Smith, predicted the Civil War in the United States. In 1832, he said that South Carolina would start a war of the South against the North and later call on Great Britain for help. (All which came true, although rumblings of tensions between the North and South date back to the 1830s and earlier.)

Words to Understand

Famine: Severe shortage of food.

Perimeter: The measurement showing distance around a two-dimensional shape.

Predict: Tell the future.

Vatican: The official residence of the pope and the administrative center of the papacy.

The Scientific Take:
Lucky Guesses or Interpretation of Life Events

Many prophecies have seemed to come true over time, but many more have not come true. Science may explain these predictions as an "odds game." When many predictions are made, a certain number are bound to come true. An article in *Popular Science* said that presentiment—an ability to anticipate something that might happen in the future—could be based on physiological cues that biology still can't explain. Prophecies are usually about events far in the future, but some who seem to predict later events may be basing their visions on the path current history appears to be taking.

Prophecies from the Mother Mary

In 1846, high in the French Alps in the town of La Salette, Melanie Mathieu (age 14) and Maximin Giraud (age 11) said that the Mother Mary appeared before them as they were minding cows and warned them of a serious **famine**. The European Potato Failure devastated the continent during this period known as the Hungry Forties and tens of thousands perished. Also, a well appeared where the children saw the apparition of Mary, and reportedly several blind people who bathed their eyes in these waters regained their sight.

On May 13, 1917, three Portuguese shepherd children had a vision of the Virgin Mary and they were told three prophecies. Believers think the first foretold World War I and the start of World War II. The second predicted the collapse of the Soviet Union and communism. The final vision was not revealed by the **Vatican** until 2000. It was interpreted to predict the assassination attempt on Pope John Paul II. The Church statement said that it appeared evident to His Holiness that it was a "motherly hand which guided the bullet's path," enabling the "dying Pope" to halt "at the threshold of death."

More about doomsday prophecies.

In some religions, the Mother of God is viewed as an almost divine being in her own right.

False Prophets

Throughout history, there have also been those who have falsely claimed to have the gift of prophecy. The Bible warns people to be wary of these false prophets or false messiahs. Determining who is a true prophet can be a difficult thing, but throughout time there have been those who have made predictions or prophecies that have not come true. Here are a few who have been labeled as false prophets:

Charles Piazzi Smyth (1819–1900) was an astronomer and scientist from Scotland who closely studied and measured the Pharaoh Khufu's Great Pyramid of Giza in Egypt in the

Charles Piazzi Smyth, an astronomer from Scotland, firmly believed that the Pharaoh Khufu's Great Pyramid in Giza, Egypt, was created with divine assistance.

1860s. His measurement of every surface and dimension turned out to be very accurate, but Smyth believed that the precision and mathematics behind the pyramid could only be explained by God. For example, the **perimeter** measurement corresponded to the number of days in the solar year.

He was convinced that the pyramid was so perfect that it had to have come from divine inspiration. He believed that the pyramid was a prophecy in stone—it not only held the secrets of world history, but it also somehow showed that the British were descended from the lost tribe of Israel.

Many Christian leaders accepted Smyth's theories and thought that the Great Pyramid had prophetic meaning. In 1924, the engineer David Davidson published the book *The Great Pyramid, Its Divine Message*. He had set out to disprove Smyth's theories, but instead he wound up embracing them and believing that the pyramids predicted that the world would end in August of 1953.

Edgar Whisenant (1932–2001) was a NASA engineer and avid Bible student. He made a prophecy that the Rapture was coming in 1988. The Rapture is thought to be the transporting of believers to Heaven when Jesus Christ returns to Earth. Whisenant became extremely wealthy when his book *88 Reasons Why the Rapture Will Occur in 1988* sold more than four million copies. Thousands even quit their jobs to prepare for the Rapture based on Whisenant's prophecy, which of course never came true.

CHAPTER 5

FAITH HEALING

In the Bible, Jesus performs many miracles, including healing the sick, lame, and blind.

It's only natural to turn to prayer and faith when someone is sick. Turning to a higher power for help in a time of crisis is common to most religions. Many Native American religions have prayers for healing. For some people, their belief in God is so strong that they think that faith alone can heal illness and other problems. Instead of medical treatment, their prayers appear to cure them. Jesus was said to have healed the sick, the lame, and the blind. He even raised a man from the dead. Since that time, many accounts of people have been told who have discovered healing through prayers and faith.

The Scientific Take: Mind Over Matter

Among some scientific circles, it is believed that the mind can have an **uncanny** power over the body and help it heal. Norman Vincent Peale, who wrote *The Power of Positive Thinking* in the 1950s, certainly believed this. He recounted a tale in his book of a man with a tumor who seemed to wish away the affliction with prayer and positive thinking. Many investigations have shown how the mind can influence the body. Hypnotherapy has been used successfully to treat irritable bowel syndrome (IBS) and other conditions. Stress can lead to inflammation of the cells. With so many mind-over-body effects proven to be true, the power of prayer and faith to heal may be scientifically tied to this phenomenon.

Words to Understand

Incision: A surgical cut in the skin.

Shrine: A holy or sacred place.

Pilgrim: A person who journeys to a sacred place for religious purposes.

Uncanny: Strange or mysterious.

Where Miracles Cure the Sick

As the story goes, on February 11, 1858, in Lourdes, France, a vision of Mary appeared before a 14-year-old girl named Bernadette Soubirous. It was the first of 18 visitations the girl would have from this "Lady in White." During her ninth vision, Soubirous said that Mary asked her to drink from the spring. There was no spring in plain sight, so she began to dig with her bare hands in the mud. Eventually, a trickle appeared, followed by a gush of water. Mary asked her to have a chapel built on this site. It would be a place where the sick could come and show their faith in God's mercy. Since that time, Lourdes has become one of the most beloved **shrines** for Catholics and million of pilgrims have come to show their faith. Thousands are said to have been healed by the waters here.

Almost 7,000 cures have been documented at the waters of Lourdes. The first was that of Catherine Latapie in March of 1858. She had a type of paralysis that affected two fingers in her right hand. The very devout mother woke early one morning with an unexplainable impulse to go to Lourdes. When she arrived, she bathed her hand in a little spring water and almost immediately her hand returned to normal. She could easily flex her fingers. That night, she returned home and gave birth to her third child who grew up to be a priest.

More recently, the Catholic Church officially recognized a miracle in the summer of 2013. The healing itself occurred on May 4, 1989, when Mrs. Danila Castelli was experiencing severe spikes in blood pressure. She visited sacred baths at Lordes on this date and emerged with "an extraordinary feeling of well-being." Her chronic health problem had been cured.

Miracles from Mother Teresa

On September 4, 2016, Mother Teresa was made a saint by the Catholic Church. Up until her death on September 5, 1997, the Catholic nun devoted much of her life to helping the poor in India. In 1979, she won the Noble Peace Prize for her efforts. Two miracles of healing have been attributed to Mother Teresa, and they sealed her sainthood with the Vatican. In the first miracle, an Indian woman with a tumor in her abdomen held a locket containing Mother Teresa's image to her stomach. The woman swore she saw a light emanate from the locket and shortly thereafter she was cured. Authorities in India have challenged the claim saying that medical treatment cured the woman.

The second miracle attributed to Mother Teresa occurred in Santos, Brazil. A local man had a serious viral brain infection and lapsed into a coma. His wife prayed over and over to Mother Teresa for help. On the day he was about to undergo an emergency operation, he woke without pain and made a full recovery. A more scientific explanation may be that his extensive drug treatment cured him.

Mother Teresa was always grateful for the support she received from the community.

Laying On of Hands

Various cultures around the world use the laying on of hands as part of their religious practices. The custom is often performed by a religious leader to heal the sick or injured. Certain scientific circles explain the effectiveness as "therapeutic touch." Practitioners believe that touching can increase the body's energy and help communication between cells. Ancient cultures in India and China believed that the body has energy fields. In traditional Chinese medicine, this energy is called qi (pronounced "chee"), whereas in India it is called prana. These energy fields may

Used in various cultures, the laying on of hands is described as being similar to a form of therapy.

be aided by touch and restore a person to good health.

Certain people have been known to have inexplicable faith healing abilities. After preaching in South Africa for decades, Reverend Reinhard Bonnke, who continues to preach today, became famous for using his faith to help heal. Many who have attended his sermons claim they have been cured of everything from AIDS to cancer to paralysis. In one of the most widely told stories, witnesses say they saw the resurrection of Daniel Ekechukwu, a Nigerian man whose wife brought his body to a church where Bonnke was talking. Bonnke has firmly said that this is true and cannot be denied.

On August 9, 1987, three-year-old Audrey Marie Santo was found nearly drowned in her family's pool in Worcester, MA. From that day, she lived her life mute and paralyzed until she died 20 years later. When miracles supposedly occurred in her bedroom (such as icons weeping blood or oil), people wanted to come visit her and pray. Several swear that their prayers at Little Audrey's bedside led to their recovery of illness. One woman with late-stage breast cancer improved after her visit to Audrey. Her oncologist, however, said her recovery was due to medication she had begun taking.

Faith healers—the showmanship and possible forces at work.

Surgeon with a Rusty Knife

One of the more dramatic stories of faith healing is that of Zé Arigo, who acquired the nickname "Surgeon with the Rusty Knife." Growing up in Brazil, he occasionally had strange hallucinations in which he would see a blinding light and hear odd voices speaking to him. As a young man, he worked in the iron mines and as a bar manager.

He lived a fairly ordinary life until 1950 when he was about 30 years old. He began to suffer strong headaches, insomnia, hallucinations, and trances. He had dreams of being in an operating room. There was a doctor in his dream who identified himself as Dr. Adolpho Fritz. He told Arigo that he was a surgeon during World War I, but his work had been cut short when he was killed. He wanted Arigo to help him by continuing his work on Earth.

Shortly thereafter, Arigo stayed in a hotel with a colleague of his, Lucio Bittencourt, an activist fighting for the rights of miners. Although Arigo did not know it, Bittencourt had cancer. After Bittencourt had fallen asleep one night, he was awoken by Arigo, who was standing before him with a glazed look in his eyes and holding a razor. Oddly, Bittencourt said he wasn't afraid as Arigo spoke to him in a German accent. Bittencourt fell unconscious and awoke with bloody pajamas. He told Arigo what had happened, but he had no memory of the incident. Bittencourt now also had an **incision** toward the back of his rib cage. When he went to be officially X-rayed, doctors discovered that his tumor had been removed.

Arigo had apparently channeled Dr. Fritz. He then decided that it was his mission to help people by performing surgery. For the next six years, he saw as many as 300 people a day in a "clinic" that he ran in his house and later in a vacant church. Before performing surgery, he would always say the Lord's Prayer, believing he was doing the work of God. In 1956, he was convicted of illegally practicing medicine, but Arigo only thought he was trying to help the poor the best he could. To his credit, he did cure many people.

Series Glossary

Affliction: Something that causes pain or suffering.

Afterlife: Life after death.

Anthropologist: A professional who studies the origin, development, and behavioral aspects of human beings and their societies, especially primitive societies.

Apparition: A ghost or ghostlike image of a person.

Archaeologist: A person who studies human history and prehistory through the excavation of sites and the analysis of artifacts and other physical remains found.

Automaton: A person who acts in a mechanical, machinelike way as if in trance.

Bipolar disorder: A mental condition marked by alternating periods of elation and depression.

Catatonic: To be in a daze or stupor.

Celestial: Relating to the sky or heavens.

Charlatan: A fraud.

Chronic: Continuing for a long time; used to describe an illness or medical condition generally lasting longer than three months.

Clairvoyant: A person who claims to have a supernatural ability to perceive events in the future or beyond normal sensory contact.

Cognition: The mental action or process of acquiring knowledge and understanding through thought, experience, and the senses.

Déjà vu: A sensation of experiencing something that has happened before when experienced for the first time.

Delirium: A disturbed state of mind characterized by confusion, disordered speech, and hallucinations.

Dementia: A chronic mental condition caused by brain disease or injury and characterized by memory disorders, personality changes, and impaired reasoning.

Dissociative: Related to a breakdown of mental function that normally operates smoothly, such as memory and consciousness. Dissociative identity disorder is a mental Trauma: A deeply distressing or disturbing experience.

Divine: Relating to God or a god.

Ecstatic: A person subject to mystical experiences.

Elation: Great happiness.

Electroencephalogram (EEG): A test that measures and records the electrical activity of the brain.

Endorphins: Hormones secreted within the brain and nervous system that trigger a positive feeling in the body.

ESP (extrasensory perception): An ability to communicate or understand outside of normal sensory capability, such as in telepathy and clairvoyance.

Euphoria: An intense state of happiness; elation.

Hallucinate: To experience a perception of something that seems real but is not actually present.

Immortal: Living forever.

Inhibition: A feeling that makes one self-conscious and unable to act in a relaxed and natural way.

Involuntary: Not subject to a person's control.

Karma: A Buddhist belief that whatever one does comes back—a person's actions can determine his or her reincarnation.

Levitate: To rise in the air by supernatural or magical power.

Malevolent: Evil.

Malignant: Likely to grow and spread in a fast and uncontrolled way that can cause death.

Mayhem: Chaos.

Mesmerize: To hold someone's attention so that he or she notices nothing else.

Mindfulness: A meditation practice for bringing one's attention to the internal and external experiences occurring in the present moment.

Monolith: A giant, single upright block of stone, especially as a monument.

Motivational: Designed to promote a willingness to do or achieve something.

Motor functions: Muscle and nerve acts that produce motion. Fine motor functions include writing and tying shoes; gross motor functions are large movements such as walking and kicking.

Mystics: People who have supernatural knowledge or experiences; they have a supposed insight into spirituality and mysteries transcending ordinary human knowledge.

Necromancy: An ability to summon and control things that are dead.

Neurological: Related to the nervous system or neurology (a branch of medicine concerning diseases and disorders of the nervous system).

Neuroplasticity: The ability of the brain to form and reorganize synaptic connections, especially in response to learning or experience, or following injury.

Neuroscientist: One who studies the nervous system

Neurotransmitters: Chemicals released by nerve fibers that transmit signals across a synapse (the gap between nerve cells).

Occult: Of or relating to secret knowledge of supernatural things.

Olfactory: Relating to the sense of smell.

Out-of-body experience: A sensation of being outside one's body, floating above and observing events, often when unconscious or clinically dead.

Papyrus: A material prepared in ancient Egypt from the pithy stem of a water plant, used to make sheets for writing or painting on, rope, sandals, and boats.

Paralysis: An inability to move or act.

Paranoid: Related to a mental condition involving intense anxious or fearful feelings and thoughts often related to persecution, threat, or conspiracy.

Paranormal: Beyond the realm of the normal; outside of commonplace scientific understanding.

Paraphysical: Not part of the physical word; often used in relation to supernatural occurrences.

Parapsychologist: A person who studies paranormal and psychic phenomena.

Parapsychology: Study of paranormal and psychic phenomena considered inexplicable in the world of traditional psychology.

Phobia: Extreme irrational fear.

Physiologist: A person who studies the workings of living systems.

Precognition: Foreknowledge of an event through some sort of ESP.

Premonition: A strong feeling that something is about to happen, especially something unpleasant.

Pseudoscience: Beliefs or practices that may appear scientific, but have not been proven by any scientific method.

Psychiatric: Related to mental illness or its treatment.

Psychic: Of or relating to the mind; often used to describe mental powers that science cannot explain.

Psychokinesis: The ability to move or manipulate objects using the mind alone.

Psychological: Related to the mental and emotional state of a person.

PTSD: Post-traumatic stress disorder is a mental health condition triggered by a terrifying event.

Repository: A place, receptacle, or structure where things are stored.

Resilient: Able to withstand or recover quickly from difficult conditions.

Resonate: To affect or appeal to someone in a personal or emotional way.

Schizophrenia: A severe mental disorder characterized by an abnormal grasp of reality; symptoms can include hallucinations and delusions.

Skeptic: A person who questions or doubts particular things.

Spectral: Ghostly.

Spiritualism: A religious movement that believes the spirits of the dead can communicate with the living.

Stimulus: Something that causes a reaction.

Subconscious: The part of the mind that we are not aware of but that influences our thoughts, feelings, and behaviors.

Sumerians: An ancient civilization/people (5400–1750 BCE) in the region known as Mesopotamia (modern day Iraq and Kuwait).

Synapse: A junction between two nerve cells.

Synthesize: To combine a number of things into a coherent whole.

Telekinesis: Another term for psychokinesis. The ability to move or manipulate objects using the mind alone.

Telepathy: Communication between people using the mind alone and none of the five senses.

Uncanny: Strange or mysterious.

Further Resources

Websites

Who Are Our Guardian Angels?/Catholic Online: www.catholic.org/saints/angels/guardian.php
Discussion of the heavenly spirit assigned by God to watch over each of us during our lives.

Blood, Gender and Power in Christianity and Judaism: Stigmata: www2.kenyon.edu/Depts/Religion/Projects/
Reln91/Blood/Christianity/stigmata.htm
This site gives an introduction to stigmata as well as examples.

Christian Medical Fellowship: Demon Possession and Mental Illness: www.cmf.org.uk/resources/publications/
content/?context=article&id=619
This organization offers one Christian perspective on distinguishing demonic possession from a mental disorder, such as schizophrenia.

Catholic Prophecy: catholicprophecy.org
A review of predictions from saints and mystics.

Practicing Our Faith: www.practicingourfaith.org/healing
This site discusses the power of healing from a Christian faith perspective.

Movies

Wings of Desire
This German film by Wim Wenders imagines a world where invisible angels listen to the thoughts of humans and comfort those who are in distress.

Leap of Faith
A Steve Martin comedy about a bogus faith healer.

Further Reading

Bell, James Stuart. *Angels, Miracles, and Heavenly Encounters: Real-Life Stories of Supernatural Events*. Minneapolis, MN: Bethany House Publishers, 2012.

Heschel, Abraham. *The Prophets (Perennial Classics)*. New York City: Harper Perennial Modern Classics, 2001.

Jeremiah, Dr. David. Angels: *Who They Are and How They Help—What the Bible Reveals*. New York: Random House, 2009.

Koenig, Harold and Malcolm McConnell. *The Healing Power of Faith: How Belief and Prayer Can Help You Triumph over Disease*. New York: Simon & Schuster, 2001.

Levack, Brian P. *The Devil Within: Possession & Exorcism in the Christian West*. New Haven, CT: Yale University Press, 2013.

Randi, James. *The Faith Healers*. Amherst, NY: Prometheus Books, 1989.

About the Author

Don Rauf has written more than 30 nonfiction books, including *Killer Lipstick and Other Spy Gadgets, Simple Rules for Card Games, Psychology of Serial Killers: Historical Serial Killers, The French and Indian War, The Rise and Fall of the Ottoman Empire*, and *George Washington's Farewell Address*. He has contributed to the books *Weird Canada* and *American Inventions*. He lives in Seattle with his wife, Monique, and son, Leo.

Index